IMMERSIONS
'THE OCEAN'

THE POETRY OF SCHIZOPHRENIA AND PSYCHOSIS

VOLUME 3

SHAKIL A I DAWOOD

KINDLE DIRECT PUBLISHING

Shakil Ahmed Ismail Dawood has been living in London for almost five decades and is now fifty-eight years of age. Schooled in Balham, South West London, and went to university in the capital, graduating in Environmental Studies and Geography.

Later he studied counselling therapy. He has suffered from schizophrenia since the age of eighteen, but the onset of symptoms he can trace back to his fourteenth year.

He was sectioned under the Mental Health Act in 1979. He lists his other interests as serious music, world literature and visual art.

Shakil witnesses calamity and difficulty not as obstacles but stepping stones to significance, meaning and success.

This book is dedicated to my colleague Grace, may she go far in her studies and beautiful accomplishment; to my manager Carolina, may she blossom wherever she goes and to my friend Karina for her beautiful intention to serve the afflicted.

INTRODUCTION

This volume of 'Immersions' finds me essentially in the same artistic mood I was in when I wrote the earlier volumes.

There is a search for implicit meaning and significance within the experience of the malady, if one chances to develop schizophrenia and/or psychosis, and a look at the condition as implicitly embodying success: success, if one takes the experience well.

My essential message to the world is that the institution of willpower, together with goodwill goes a long way to rehabilitate the client as a most important member of society, even though the illness may not recede in its workings.

But the client is one of the most important members of society at the onset of the condition, and in its conflagration.

Shakil Ahmed Ismail Dawood,

London. Edited 31st July 2019.

KINDLE DIRECT PUBLISHING

IMMERSIONS
'THE OCEAN'

THE POEMS

<u>TRYING</u>

Trying is the most important,
Critical step on this stage
And you can try – always -
What-so-ever life's ague:

However, trying is the finest,
Trying's essential to bring along
That with hard work is spanner
To undo schizophrenia's wrong:

Trying is to set up hope,
And a great future beget,
To catch the fish of the
Humane in good intentions' net:

Trying is to man-up
To drink the bitter wine,
Wine eventually leading to
Drunkeness sublime:

To try is to near, approach
The indispensable beginning
Trying's enacting the nature
That can begin again, living:

For, the rock-like mountain
Of being is truly shattered,
When you by schizophrenia
Are life-removed and scattered:

But, being blown to bits
To smaller pieces of rock,
The rock-mountain becomes
Many a shaped building block:

Your patience the mortar,
Your goodwill the crane,
With virtue's great strength
You start re-building from bane:

A majestic edifice, monument
Is now being brilliantly built,
When responsible, you feel
More settled, though like silt:

Now, with every license
To realize, and leave hell,
The world looking on
Is cast into a wondrous spell:

It's the heart magnified
Which is the ticket, the fee,
And courage, and patience
And hope the universal key:

Trying alone, is great,
Is departure peer-less,
Trying in its own right
Is success beyond success:

What then, when success
Isn't actual, really manifest?
Even in this case you're topmost
All trying takes you to the crest:

Failure after trying means
That you can still be serene,
Success has come anyway
Triumph in your inward seen:

Trying is in the void,
Building in the unseen,
It is the unseen heavens
Most beautiful scene:

I tried, sincerely so, and
The breeze came my way,
Bringing news from heaven,
Congratulations to say:

Which also said, you tried,
Against the greatest odds,
In trying, you chose the finest
From the Divine and heaven's lots:

The heavens salute you,
And you're duly saluted,
In great, exalted company
Accompanied and feted:

Sufferers! Try! Try! Trying
Is travelling swiftly: why,
Your humanity's most sublime
When you trying imbibe and imply:

The poet John Keats said:
'I'd sooner fail, than not try.'
You've put, by trying, blessing
Into hearts, into the world and sky.

THE KEY TO TREASURE

The great truth is,
That struck down, felled
By schizophrenia,
I did my best
I tried hard – very hard

Under every duress,
And every difficulty,
I did my best,
Even if it was as little as
Returning to hope
After utter despair,
After another devastating
Capitulation,
On another onerous day

I always had in mind
That I had to work
And work hard
To bear with this nemesis
And yes, though I veered
From the set track of hard work
And doing one's best
On many occasions,

This effort,
And its necessity
Always hovered in my conscience

The greatest trial I faced
Was conditioning myself
To the inward scarring,
And habituate myself
To the presence in my heart
Of an inner world undone

But I regarded this turning over
Of my inner universe
As a ploughing –
For me to sow seeds,
With hope as the sowing action

I knew, forty years ago,
Finally, with certitude
That it was a tremendous battle
I was engaged in,
For all my talents
Had been rendered fallow

And this certitude
Came bearing down on me
With grave weight
After a catastrophic relapse in 1987
Now not only were my talents dormant,
The harvest of my patience
Over the previous eight years
Was consigned to oblivion

And I was left with one recourse
Love – and goodness
Love for God,
Man,

And nature -
And goodwill
Towards all creation

And loving and good,
Something precious happened to me
I completely lost
All propensity for bitterness
Henceforth,
Under the two-fold umbrella
Of Love and goodness,
I never ever became bitter

And losing this propensity
For dissatisfaction,
I laid the foundations
Of a satisfied personality
Though, in the interim,
I had a great battle to wage

It would take me another three decades
After the debacle of 1987
To reach satisfaction,

Acceptance of my losses,
But being free of bitterness
Was the key to my success,
Though it took a long time
For my long-term strategy
To register in my personality
But, 'better late than never'

And hence, I conclude –

If there is any condition
The person with chronic schizophrenia
Needs to instil
Within their heart,

It is a sweet disposition
To thus never give oneself the need
To express,
Or feel,
Bitterness

This is a key to treasure
For, what awaits the client
At the terminus
Is treasure of personality
And character,
And a great achievement!

I achieved this momentous outcome
Doing my best,
And working hard,
Little knowing
That at the initial moment
I decided upon industry
And sincerity,
That such treasure lay ahead of me!

It was the treasure of peace-of-mind,
An onerous conscience laid to rest,
And a triumph at the management
Of the impossible.

Such worthwhile journeys
Are only undertaken by the fortunate,
And hence I say
That schizophrenia and psychosis
Were my good fortune!

<u>HARBOUR......</u>

Conflagration
One that fierily burns
The whole house down,
And the awaited surrender
To schizophrenia
Are events that have
To be kept at bay

They are the inmost breach
Of all that constitutes a human being
The sanctity of a human being
Is very successfully transgressed
And you're totally, utterly disarmed,
Disempowered with a vengeance

What I needed now,
From society,
Was to be garlanded

And I was
By kind psychiatric nurses,
And lovely support staff –

Inhaling the fragrance of the blooms
Around me,
Bestowed so generously
And kindly,
I resolved upon the battle
Of rebuilding
Rebuilding my resurrection

I was 'common' and 'elect'
At the same time
I was 'common'
Because
I'd been completely reduced
As a 'viable' personality,
And 'elect'
Because in my utterly
dishevelled state,

I warranted in the eyes of nurses
And support staff
And deserved
In their hearts
Their utmost care
And consideration

In the finest garlanding

And adorning
Possible to a human being,
And my heart enfolded
A series of valuable traits

I elected to be patient,
Kind and loving
Beautiful strident voices
That would have an echoing call,
A sound that would restore me,
Way beyond nominal uplifting
I was to become a thinker,
Contributing to imaginative thought,

And adding to the beauty in the world

Yes, with the support of nurses,
And mental health support staff,
I would transcend the meaning
Of resurrection, and unfolding
Into viable success

Their indefatigable support for me
Was the harbour
My rudderless, sail-less boat
Docked in

For repairs directed by myself

To resort to love and
Kindness And support
From these beautiful people in tow,
I achieved a tacit self-absolving
One I did not speak about,
For it was a deepening of me,
The depths my returning nature
Was reaching was hitherto uncharted
And so, I strove in silence,
Purely intent.
(And today I strive,
purely intent).

The harbour of these supportive,
And great people,
Initiated my implacable resolve,
And enabled the able exposition

Of my ability to wage battle
When I saw the beauty
And greatness of their vocation
And its tremendous hope and
Wonderful intentions
My fellow sufferers

There is a harbour that exists
For your bedraggled ship
Of post-hospital existence
If you're fortunate enough
Lucky enough, to receive it –

The support of sincere,
Kind and considerate
Mental health workers –
Then, having repaired your ship,
You can leave the dock
For the greatest journey
You will possibly undertake
The journey to a new self –
Your very own self!

<u>UNVEILED AND THEN</u>
<u>THE VEILING (1979)</u>...

1979

I can now,
Easily be surmised
As easily worthy
Of being dismissed
By most lay people

I was never an open book
My personality and character
Open and clear to read,
And fully fathom
There was always,
Something of the enigmatic in me,
And even then,
People could really only manage to
Take a cursory glance at me
I managed to remain,
Effortlessly,
A mystery
As significant,
And meaningful
But now,

The depth in me is gone,
My layers of veils
Of traits, and qualities
And my nature
My personality
And character
Coverings over my reality,
That kept me a secret
And hence in a way,
Vital and critical
And viable
Have been subsumed,
Dissolved and absorbed,
Not I think, by the malady,
But by its medical treatment.

The real me is lost, somewhere,
And is untraceable,
And cannot be re-enacted,
And I can now be equalled
By most people –
I, who once blazed a trail
Of individuality

And uniqueness
And brilliance

The real me it is now impossible
To re-fashion and re-make

Nor, with the inner abortion,
Am I left with anything to say,
My inward is opaque,
Dense,
And occluded
The fluidity and 'flexibility'
Of personality,
Character
And intellect
Is one solid, insignificant
Inner edifice,
Which is taken, and read,
And understood
In one glance
And dismissed

I am no longer complex -
Vital and critical, that is.

And how will this solidified,
Densest of inner worlds
Once again become truly living
How will life be brought

To un-living stone?

How will I, once again,
Speak, with gravity,
Articulately,
Relating
A flourishing inward
To the world?

How will I once again,
Draw the covers
Over my personality,
Character
And intellect,
And veil myself
Into significance again?

I do not know–
I do not know.

But I can sow seeds
Though I fully know
That the stony field
That I am now
Cannot be ploughed,
And is, to all purposes, barren.

But I didn't know
That I possessed plough,
And clover
And watering
All in one
In my sincerity
Sincerely,
I decide to keep Love
In my heart
Even though,
Right now,
And in the foreseeable future,
Disabled now,
I won't be able
To convey and show that Love.

I sincerely meant my sincerity,
Which then had the built in practice
Of patience.
Eight years later:

I am a graduate,
I have genuine personality,
Real character,
And authentic intellect

There is a mask of goodwill
Over me –
I am an enigma once more,
No longer an 'open book',
To be fathomed,
And then dismissed.
No I am real,
And authentic
And significant
And meaningful
In anybody's book.

I have managed
To veil myself again.

Sincerity,
Goodwill
And patience
Are right now,
Given the medical model
That treats schizophrenia,
The only true reaction
Of meaning to it.
The medical model
Utterly, detrimentally,
Unveils people like me –

Sincerity,
Patience
And goodwill
Restores the veils.

I am no longer an open book.
My enigmatic nature,
My inner edifice,
Re-created,
Is replete with meaning
And significance –
Moreover with that mostly salutary
And benevolent

And I bring the feeling of peace
With me where-ever I go –
My personality
Shows its intelligence:

Is it not worthwhile
Being sincere,
Patient,
And of good will
When struck down
By the implacable nemesis
Of schizophrenia?

<u>HEART BROKEN?</u>

Can anybody not witness?

You are all around me,
Yet you do not read
Into my presence

You do not witness
That I have great responsibility –
For diplomacy
All over the world

Every war-torn zone
Is relying on me
For its salvation
And resolution

And these wars are so terrible
So bloody,
And genocidal

And so, my responsibility
Is an onerous and great one

But woe is me!

I visualized an end to one war
But I did not write my salving
Conclusions down
And I have thus lost the content
Of my deliberations

Woe is me,
I, who could have saved
millions of lives,
But because I have been remiss,
And irresponsible,
Slaughter has reigned

And it is my fault.

How will I live now,
How can I live now?
My conscience will afflict me
Forever now...

Just as one difficulty
A love lost,
Is redeemed
By another love,
One horror
In the experience of schizophrenia

Is replaced by another
And so I moved,
Indeed developed away
From the above catastrophe
To another
I have committed,
Of equal grandeur and scale...

But I am not heart broken,
Despite the tremendous level
At which my original misdemeanour
Was perpetrated –
Somehow, deep, deep within me,
I witness hope and salvation –
For all and everything in the world.
For me this is experience of Beauty –

Somehow, deep within me,
All is OK,
All over the world,
And myself –
Does not the world,
Including myself
Have an immense destiny,
One that is certain to be realized?
And this thought gives me catharsis

And solace and comfort.

My reason for narrating the above
Is that no matter how sick a person is,
With schizophrenia –
Or any other mental illness,
Deep, deep within them
There is a beautiful place –
A locus of succour
And sustenance
In hour of the be-devilry
Of mental illness –

To this region of Beauty
Does the client turn,
Consciously,
Or usually, unconsciously
To yet keep a foothold on viability
And vitality –
An ongoing life
That can yet successfully transact life

This is why the perceived horror
Of one's suspected awry conduct
Does not perturb lastingly
And one smoothly alights

on another 'horror'
To occupy oneself,
And the original blight disappears.

There is beauty,
The partaking of the existence
Of a real inner beauty,

In smoothly moving from one
Symptom to another,
And losing the disturbing contents
Of the first.

There is then in the depths
Of the heart
Of the client
A beautiful resource,
A wonderful recourse
That is the finest asset
In the hour of his or her severe
Tribulation.

In this lies that indispensable necessity –
The client's hope.

AWARENESS AND SCHIZOPHRENIA

You're aware of its malevolence
The ripe sourness,
The distilled acrid nature,
The starvation of sensibility,
Your key-less presence
Outside the fortress gate of denial -
But are you truly aware of it?

This is the question to ask:

Are you aware of its dynamic constancy,
Always in your heart's orbit,
Desiring ransack?

Are you aware of its graphic,
perennial vision
To insert a habitual suffering,
To reduce your heart's gravity
Its constant desire to outwit you?
You're unconscious of this awareness.
For good reason.

So conscious are you to portray
ultimate enmity

To this beguiling nemesis
That of good character
That you forget its whereabouts
in your midst
It is coursing through your veins –

And this unconsciousness
is imperative,
For you need holistic answers
To an all-encompassing dilemma.

And good character, an absorbing,
Emphatic resolution of
sacrosanct heart,
And a mind made to will thus,
Is the first and last occupation,

Of a being occupied by schizophrenia
Goodness is all permeating,
All-embracing.
Goodness is the first and last stage
Of consciousness –
And being so,
it precludes all awareness
Of the strength and fortitude
Of an enemy desiring to unfold itself

Yet again-
Yet again.

And then, I emphasise
Love and kindness
In tandem with goodwill
I fight back, unconscious
Of the hovering of schizophrenia,
Ready to pounce, fangs bared
And I do not possess
the spare energy
To also attend to it.

This is a humane repartee
to this condition.
And humanity is a blanket prescription
To all ills and ailments

It does not matter then,
That you're not fully aware of
schizophrenia
In your very fibre,
In your pith and marrow
You're absolved of this
need and duty,
Because of your preoccupation

With goodness,
Kindness and love
And all this,
Despite living schizophrenia!

FATE'S GREATEST DIRECTOR......

While schizophrenia writes
Articulately,
And in novel fashion
Onto your personality,
And onto your quality of intellect,
Putting both into stasis,
And instils an aspiration
That cannot be equalled
In pain, sorrow and hurt,
It also ably paves the way
To your destiny
An unlimited, vast destiny –

You began as an ocean,
Teeming with life –
The life of ideas
And creativity
And able abilities
In science,
Now the tide is out,
And the ocean that teemed

Is not to be seen
It seems to have evaporated
Into nothingness

Schizophrenia
Has brought in a pre-condition
That will – or it seems will be –
Your condition,
Perpetually,
Perennially
Your fate seems decided,
Decisively,
Decidedly so
That the doldrums
Is all the ocean that you were
Will be henceforth

But I knew something,
Something great
Very great
That would address waters
Far away in the distance
And call them
To the shore of your being,

Once again teeming
With ideas,
Creativity
And insight into science
And this great quality
Is patience!

Naturally sincere,
And a makeup that wished well,
And possessing goodwill,
It was a four-pronged call
To my ocean to billow again,
Surge back

A decade of patience,
And the ocean of my being
Arrived back, allowing me
To set sail
Any ship of imagination
And desire I desired –

And this ocean,
Lying in the doldrums
For so long,

Had been unadulterated
In its exile,
And came back with a pure spirit,
Also making my spirituality
Of consequence and meaning –

All round then,
In the sciences,
The arts
And spirituality,
I was a winner –
Winning with aplomb!

I have made you witness
Fate's greatest director –
None other
Than schizophrenia!

It seems improbable, does it not,
That this forbidding,
Destructive condition
Should be the forerunner
Of such personal meaning,

Consequence
And significance?
But this is what patience constitutes
When struck with this malady
Patience, in total,
And when assisted
by virtuous tendency
Converts a constant desire
For destroying and malevolence
Into a gateway
That ushers in a beautiful state,
A wonderful dynamism,
Lovely thought,
Well meant speech
And the kindest actions

The indelible imagery
Of original schizophrenia
This grave malady,
Given license by patience
Transforms itself into a director

Of the wondrous,
he miraculous
Something brought into being
That cannot be bettered:
Is not schizophrenia,
Taken well,
Allowed to be fate's
Greatest director?

A GREATER LIFE...

I was once enthusiastic
About the mind –

Imagination,
Insight,
Parallels
And creativity

I felt living,
And my mind felt alive

And this enthusiasm
Was self-elicited,
Self-sustaining

Then came the blight
Of illness,
Which the current system,
Given its talents,
Abilities
And knowledge,
Could not but mismanage

And I could not locate my mind
Anymore
It could no longer be felt
By my senses

In conversation,
I could not feel
That I'd fittingly conversed,
With any meaning
Or feeling

Bereft now,
I couldn't analyse,
I couldn't imagine vividly
And was absolutely stripped
Of the insightful capacity,
The faculty to create
Had by-passed me

I thought
Or truly felt
That I had no intellect

The blazing flame
Of an ardent mind's abilities
Was now extinguished,

And I encountered my intellect
What remained of it
As an aborted intellect
A dead intellect

But death is a seed
Greater than the seed
Or a rose
Or any seed
That gives issue to the valuable

And the seed of death
Is watered by waters
More precious than rainfall
Is shone upon
By a sun
Greater than the cosmic sun

Patience!

And so,
My intelligence,
Buried,
With the practice of patience,
Was to establish roots,
Deep roots

And precious nascent shoots
And then, patience
Still in tow,
Was to flourish
And blossom
Into the utmost beauty

And all this,
In the wake
Of the exercise
Of patience
The lesson is,
That if you're patient-

All you've lost
Is rekindled
And replaced
With something better
Than before –

In the grave,
One is,
Or ought to be,
Naturally patient.

<u>THE OCEAN...</u>

Schizophrenia is not an ocean -
You are.

It is a drop,
That becomes a trickle,
Then a raging torrent
That enters,
Nay forces its way into the ocean
Of your personality,
Intellect,
Spirit,
And character,
And becomes the ocean –

This is you,
Thoroughly infused
With the dissolving of schizophrenia
In your shallows,
And depths,
And the entire solution
Of the ocean of you
Becomes schizophrenia.

Hence, now,
Because you *now are* schizophrenia
It is extricable from your being –
You've reached the point of no return.

This is the version, chronic,
Of the malady encapsulated:

And how, just how,
One racks one's brain,
Can one contend?

The answer is to transform
The ocean
Wholly so,
Completely
Wholesale
With good character
Goodness
Permeating, and infused
Into every facet of it

With all-embracing goodness
The depths – and shallows of
This ocean
Are brought brightness

And luminosity
Every drop of the ocean
Becomes beautiful

To make something as vast,
As huge as an ocean
A great heart,
Containing the vastness
Of personality
And character
Entirely beauteous
Is a tremendous under-taking,
And successfully realized,
Can only be the issue
Of the finest genius

So there we have it

Schizophrenia

Is an invitation
To the exercise
Of your genius
When you sincerely portray
Good character
In every facet

Of personality
In word,
Thought
And deed
Schizophrenia,
Even when it thoroughly, thoroughly,
Suffuses your entire makeup,
Is an opportunity
The great avenue
To your genius

And goodness,
Being universal brilliance,
Makes your genius in turn
Universal

You are completely,
Thoroughly accomplished

This is real alchemy
And magic
To transform
The acid ocean
Of schizophrenia
Into honey!

THE GREAT MEANING BEYOND THE SYMPTOMS OF SCHIZOPHRENIA

When schizophrenia
Invites you
To its abyss,
And you are to settle there
For a while
You have to leave all ken,
All education of yourself
Behind

Your knowledge of self,
Your abilities
Your ability to comprehend,
For example,
Your disposition,
Your manner of employing
your mind,
All remain on the outskirts
Of the present moment,
The present living

The only measure –
The only measure
Against such a debacle,
One that bodes permanence,
And a stay of longevity,
Is to retrace your steps,
But travel forwards
At the same time:
That is build yourself up
Through what you've been
In the past,
Which is what you really are,
What you embody deep within
And you resort to a forgotten past,
Now rekindled, to do this,
And vigorously take strides
Into the present.

Hence, I write this poem –

To recreate
The torn and ravelled fabric
Of my mind and heart.

I will listen to my music
Of yesteryear,

And rekindle my by-gone
Interpretation of it in the past,
And bring my past
And then myself right now,
By retracing myself,
And becoming that retracing,
Alive again.

Yes, it is death,
This schizophrenia –
Long-term death,
And many-a-time,
There has been another escapade,
Yet another dose of demise.
Cessation is injected into one
At various points in the journey,
Always unexpectedly.

But, I, even now,
Know the value of Beauty:

The Beauty of kindness:

Hence, I will be kind
Throughout the present,
As I always have been,

And thus retain a strong grasp
On the purple thread
That runs through my life,
Schizophrenia notwithstanding,
Despite this malady.

In contrast to the niggardliness
Of the condition,
Kindness, is, truly speaking,
Abundance:
I may feel shorn now,
But in kindness,
I am wealthy.

I am yet rich,
Opulent beyond my means,
And will build on this opulence,
Creating yet another chapter of
significance
And meaning for myself.

I travel then,
Through my present impasse,
By Beauty
The greatest Beauty,
The practice of kindness,

Intended,
And then conferred
As liberally as I can,
And I come back
From the abyss
Once again.
There is great meaning
Beyond the symptoms of schizophrenia,
If you take the initiative
And attempt to supplant

The substance and implications
Of the malady
With ever-fresh behaviour
That based on kindness:

Wholly refreshed from its throes,
This is a complete reversal,
A complete turnaround
Of the pulping, macerating nature
Of this condition

It attempts to make you upside-down:
Kindness bestows upon you an even keel,
An achievement so significant,

You've come back more meaningful than ever!

'The comeback makes you greater –
'Losing the championship,
'And coming back.' (Muhammad Ali)

THE ATTAINMENT AND ACHIEVEMENT: A POEM IN PROSE

You were afflicted with mental illness: you showed, quite clearly, throughout your affliction, and thereafter, an astute sensibility.

And you managed this, in-spite of, and through the fog and haze of your suffering. To possess a keen sense within the cloudiness of malady is a real and true achievement.

Mental illness blunts the sharp cutting edge of the personality and the intellect. And yet you are very personable and thoughtful – and kind and well intentioned. And this deep acquired sensibility can only be the fruit of authentic intelligence and plainly, reason.

When your mind was sealed from you, you were obedient to your heart – a good heart – and acted upon its will and desires. In the Unseen realm then – in another and yet very real world – you have passed through and beyond this one.

Mental illness is a seed planted in arid soil, in a state of drought and in conditions of darkness – and yet you've overflowed and flowered.

You have hence achieved the improbable, the impossible. And now you brim over with Love. What could be a greater attainment?

This great gain in personality, intellect and character is the meaning of thinking well, speaking well and acting well – being in possession of, and focussed on a good nature – when in the throes of mental illness and its aftermath.

A POEM IN PROSE FOR THOSE WHO HAVE SUFFERED FROM MENTAL ILLNESS

When you are aware that you are alone, remember that everyone is special – they are born special – thus, you still have real rank and stature in the world: a really special rank and a really special stature;

When you are aware that you want to achieve more, fill your moments with sincere, good great intentions, and try to act out the simpler ones.

Mere good intention alone is an actual achievement, for it is work completed in your inward, once and for all. How actually great can great good intentions make you then?

When you think that you lack vision, view the world through the prism and lens of goodness, kindness, love and forgiveness.

Your eyesight will improve and the visualizing ability of your mind and heart will be extended and heightened.

And you will cool your eyes and bring comfort to both your mind and heart;

When you are aware of disability, it is the very moment to become an intellectual – to transcend – to think, speak and act beyond disability, by being kind, which is brilliance: a complete deed by a complete being;

When you are aware that you are separated from your aspirations and ambitions, make your mark – an indelible mark on the world – by being kind: kindness being brilliance, a brilliant action, you have hence greatly achieved;

And when you are aware that you have suffered, remember that you have been through the most beautiful experience possible to a human being:

for, sorrow is the deepest emotion, and having such a depth in mind and heart, it has to be very beautiful.

Thus you have, by your experience of mental illness, been greatly beautified!

DISABILITY AND THE GOOD MENTAL HEALTH WORKER

I have played out a drama.

There is darkness in the auditorium,
The audience have left,
And I have lost the acting art
Not merely for presentation,
But even for myself

The lasts few acts
Were played out by me
Without meaning
And significance,
By any measure
Of meaning
And significance

An yet it was, in totality,
A major drama
I had engaged in;
And a solo performance.

There was no Director
After the first act,
And four major acts were due to follow
And no playwright
I was the playwright
Or, meant to be.

In the last of the scenes
The dialogue
Was within myself,
The drama was within

It was dignity,
Throughout
That drove the stage,
And the actions
Were lovingly intended
Good intentions
Which couldn't be visualized
Moreover, it was a mediocre performance
After the first act,
And the audience started leaving then:

But their leaving was a wonder
Into the greatness of the audience
The few stayed:

The more that stayed,
The greater they were,
As characters and personalities
The greatest stayed till the end
Their greatness
Was their compassion,
And tremendous
Did this learned few
Deem my performance

In reality my performance
Was great indeed –
For dignity,
When bereft of acting arts
And only possessed of loving intentions,
A triumph of meaning
And significance
Had been staged –

For this is what a hamstrung actor
With goodness
And kindness
And love
In his heart
Achieves
On life's stage.

<u>HOPE...</u>

Once, to being afflicted with
schizophrenia,
I was not at all concerned
I didn't give a straw

Brilliant, vivacious,
and in very good health,
It was beyond my imagination
I'd be made raw:

But it did not come upon me suddenly
Stalking me slowly, like the wisest foe,
It came upon me totally unsuspected,
Unfelt, unrealizable,
stealthily and slow:

It never occurred to me, once great,
That I would be reduced to poverty
Inner and outer, in my makeup,
My character owning no inward
property:

It never occurred to me that freedom
Once so liberally available to me,

Could summarily be taken away
That never again would
I ever be free:

It was an inveterate enemy
from within
Hostile, destructive,
driven in enmity,
And I was blinded, deaf and dumb
To everything – only
hope I could see:

Dishevelled now,
outrunning my existence,
And ambitions aborted and incomplete,
I couldn't do anything –
nothing at all
But I did everything with
hope see and treat:

Hounded, persecuted, and deserted,
I raised myself up, and tried still,
For I could sense ambitions and life –
All I could with hope
sustain and distil:

Never could I think ably, appropriately,
Trusting my abilities
as previously as of old,
But I believed in hope
ardently, fervently,
An immersion in the
ocean of hope un-tolled

Hope, from my prone
state and situation,
Is verily a heavenly quality,
from eternity,
That renders me tacitly,
unknown, unseen,
A major player on life's stage:
a personality:

So hope was the clearing, the cleansing,
My life and living's clean, felt ablution
It was the only great
quality I possessed
But it was salutary —
and a timely resolution:

I began slowly, reading,
and patiently
Recreating my mind:
and hope I praise
For my mind,
heart and my entire nature,
Education, vocation and leisure
it did raise:

If in my being bereft
of every knowledge,
I did yet reveal a workable
life-philosophy,
Attempting to think and speak
was the action:
Hope was the immovable foundation: the
theology:

So I stumbled upon the real religion:
Hope: the essence of Truth: so true,
It is every religion's
core and essence,
And the essential foundation
of it too:

Hope is real, *the* truthful fact of life,
If you are to win at all in
this earth's miasma,
You need to apply the real
and truthful fact
And one day you're in
charge of *your* drama!

Hope enabled me to
transcend most bounds,
It enabled my patience, to all,
the great key
You cannot buy real true
achievement – never
Hope cannot be purchased
It is beyond fee:

Hope brought me,
in the final analysis,
Education, achievement and praise,
Hope took away my blindness,

I see now,
And I had seen through
schizophrenia's haze:

My fellow children, men and women:
Don't give up –
do not give up on hope:
For when shorn by some misfortune,
The death is given an injection
of life – scope!

DISABILITY AND THE SPECIAL EYE...

In my disability,
I yet sincerely attempted
Thought

And then,
Sincerity being fully
The by-word,
And with practice
Of bitter patience,
I managed somehow
To kindle,
Not the fire of my intellect,
But mere smoke

But, in actually managing this,
Kindling mere smoke,
By actively,
Sincerely
And patiently
Acting on my aspiration
To think,

I completely know

With certitude
That there cannot be smoke
Without fire
I knew that there truly was
A raging fire
Beneath
The trickle-like
Emanation
Of the smoke
Of my mental capacities
In other words,
I had rekindled my intellect.

But,

'Beauty requires a special eye –
*'Beauty is not made for every eye.........'**
And so,
Only the great,
The very especial
Can bear witness
To my achievement!

*A line of verse by the contemporary
Pakistani poet Sajid.

SCHIZOPHRENIA AND STUDY

I was to learn,
That love
Is the universal key:

I started developing this malady
At the age of fourteen
It wasn't full blown
Until four years later
But throughout, I engaged in one
All consuming activity
And passion
That of a brilliant scholar

Then, I was 'Miser
'of sound and syllable,
'no less than Midas
'of his coinage'*

Yes, poetry engrossed me,
As a teenager,
Before the circumventing
Advent of schizophrenia;

But so did the subjects
Of the sciences
And spirituality –
In short,
I had a thirst for knowledge
Unparalleled amongst my peers;

Then, spearheading annulment,
Came schizophrenia,
Crushing all attempts to study,
My passion for studious endeavours
So pleasant,
The font of my happiness;

I'd no imagination left;
I'd no intellect left,
Let alone an intellectual faculty;
I'd lost all my knowledge;
I'd lost the feeling of well-being
And social safety
That came in tandem,
Hand in hand,

With the state of being a good scholar;
I couldn't articulate
the consummate idea,
Even if I read it thoroughly,
And tried to comprehend it;

The thriving inner world
Of the arts
Spirituality
And the sciences –
Of the competent scholar
Had been severed from me,
By a severe violence
And reduction
That stamped itself
On my every waking moment.

And so I lost my lifeline.

Losing my intellect
And personality
Hit my vulnerability

One I wasn't conscious of
Until this grave, disabling calamity.

My living became
A drama of despair,
Capitulation
And a dishevelling
That caused a pain,
A suffering
That cannot be paralleled –
It was utter deprivation,
Faced only by the most unfortunate
Among humanity.
But at this cataclysmic moment,
I decided upon something spiritual,
I said to myself,
Echoing Oscar Wilde when in prison,
'Even though I cannot show it,
'I must keep love in my heart,
'else what will happen to my soul?'

This moment saved me.
And I devolved upon patience.

I meditated,
And considered this love
And I kept in my heart
Its implications,
Even though these were now
Mere intentions,
And thus I beautified
my inner world,
Made it fecund, ploughed and fertile
To receive a garden,
Where all there now was aridity

And I emphasize my patience
Through all this.
Nine years later,
I had two university degrees.

My hard fought battle
To regain my intellect
And intellectual faculties
I cannot relinquish now;
I revel in them;
I have once again become
'Miser of sound and syllable...'

Love, then is the foundation
Of someone's dealings with
This serious, deleterious eventuality –

If you keep love in your heart,
Meditate upon its beauty
You beautify yourself –
Then, as beauty attracts beauty,
And as you exercise patience,
Your beautiful love attracts
Your beautiful intellect back to you.
You develop a wonderful personality,

And your whole world
Becomes a garden,
And everywhere you look,
You create a great bloom.
My fellow sufferers!
How much can you achieve,
If you can keep
Love in your heart,
And keep that love alive
In your heart –

And what if you're able enough
To live that love,
Express it in word
And action, how incredible
A being of potential
Will you become?
Love is the universal
Key that can open all doors,
Including, breaking down

The fortress-strong doors,
The crippling, disabling doors
And ramparts
So formidably
Instituted by schizophrenia!

*John Keats, poet.

<u>DAILY BATTLE...</u>

Daily, I face my nemesis,
Fully armoured,
Filled to the brim
To impart violence

The morning begins
With its verbal berating
And thought inroads
And then levelled
By a sharp double pronged thrust
Into your inner most being,
You are left to clear the debris,
And try to make the existence
Existence calls of you,
From your levelled inner world

But all this, my daily fight,
Has a precedent,
Harking back to its inception
As a being that is to tower
I was then fourteen years of age –

Initially, it is a slow incursion,
A slight lesson,

Thoroughly learnt,
In inner imbalance
And then it matures

Two years later, at sixteen,
You are object of the command
Of barking orders
Heard only by yourself
And it is literally, a trick,
Or magic,
How you manoeuver around these,
And witness them as implausible

It then gives itself the wildest license
To set ablaze your entire inner realm;
And then two years later,
This blaze has left ashes
as the remnants,
But with the smoke,

Heat and flames still raging –

And now, at fifty-eight, I say this
To myself daily:
Once it is inaugurated,
You are forever

At inauguration,
Combined with,
In its repeated visits,
With its refinement,
And its culture,
With a development of power,
And impetus,
Despite its visitations,
Having to recourse
To the seat of its enthronement –
Your heart –

And all its powers,
Are devoted to one end –
Assault,
Relentless assault
With an irresistible

And implacable nature

Its idea of attainment
Is unusual
Its gaze is forwards,
To more gain
In destruction
And mayhem,

Instituted both boldly
And slyly –

It is deaf,
With no ears
It cannot hear
Your remonstrations
Your screams –
And its deafness develops,
After all, does it not have to spend
A lifetime with you?

And so, you're brought up to speed –
Every-day, each morning
With its one way verbal interchange

And wit, whose thinking is linear –

And what did I do today, with all this,
Revisited as I am?

I could only think of good things
Kindness,
Goodness,
And love
I didn't have the power to speak,

Made bereft of that faculty
By violence, and battery,
And I patiently endured

Once again,
I'd planted a seed that would grow
Imminently – swiftly
Whose leafy – miraculous – growth
That would create a canopy of shade
Under schizophrenia's scorching sky
And that's about all the
relief I can expect
And I am grateful

My personality is beaten down,
But my faculty of speech slowly returns
And I can begin to think again
The mental fog is evaporating,
And this allows inner clarity

I have a semblance of being now,
And I now plan my day
A useful day
Of creating happiness for others,
By being good,
Kind and loving

I can reach again,
And I write poems.

I am now out in the open,
The world my oyster.

I will repeat today's
happenings tomorrow,
When my erstwhile nemesis
Revisits me, once again

But I have created hope today
For others, if not myself –
Through my goodness –
And so I have definitely
achieved today

And so I am satisfied with today –
And I will be, again,
Tomorrow.

HARMONY...

I need to harmonize
With mind and heart,
With my world
The world of relations,
Friends,
And strangers

I need to harmonize
With my mind,
And heart,
History,
Literature,
Science
Arts
And spirituality

I need to be at one with these
Unavoidable aspects of my world –

I was cut off,
Severed, seceded

In relationship
With my entire world
At the age of fourteen,
When this upstart condition
Embedded itself, suffusing,
Within my entire inner world –

An occlusion in relations
With everything inside
And outside myself
Established itself,
Immovably so –

I am now fifty-eight,
And have been patient, and patient,
For the past forty-four years

And this protracted patience,
Whilst it enabled the earning of laurels,
Unparalleled for those of my ilk,
Has not enabled restoration –

The harmonizing I have so desired,
A re-connection
That has innate vitality,

Meaning,
And richness –
Yes, in my subsequent conduct,
A habitual, consistent one,
I have practiced, sincerely,
Goodness,
Kindness,
And love
And truly came across
Relationships of substance,
But the original, vital,
Innate,
Integral
Feeling of consummate relationship
According to my birth-right,
Has permanently escaped me –

This is one of the strictures
Of this malady,
And whilst not my major concern
From day to day,
Hovers as a backdrop,
That is critical
To the quality of one's existence

I have learnt,
In the intervening forty-four years
Vital, critical knowledge,
But no knowing
Can re-establish the harmony,
Which now seems to forever
To inhabit in an unseen,
Unreachable universe
But could it be,
That this lack of desired amity
Between myself and the world
Is two sided?

That it simply isn't schizophrenia alone
That inaugurates estrangement,
Particularly without oneself,
With the world of people
And studies?

Could it be that it is the world
That is inadequate in its
approach to me?

I say this,
Because
I harmonize,
And have always done so,
Despite the meaning of schizophrenia,
Vitally,
Critically,
Innately,
With little children,
Animals,
Prophets
And saints –
And with as much aplomb as I desire
Why is it then that the
aspects of the world
That represent purity,
And authentic greatness,
I have always been reconciled to,
And am always in harmony with?

Is it because, now,
rendered child-like
By schizophrenia,
I am not in like-minded company?

Greatness, then,
Is to be child-like,
Or animal-like –
And I have been 'cleansed'
Of all life experiences,

Particularly after serious relapses
As an adult
And thus, I have assumed
my birthright,
To be great,
Something I achieved
By a permanent return to
a child-like nature

And so, I have reasoned out
The secession of my harmony
with the world
At least that of people
That the world of adults
Does not perceive my simple nature,
And that my studies, in their fruit,
Are simple as well

But, they say,
'Simplicity is genius'
Perhaps, schizophrenia,
In rendering me child-like,
And simple

Has made me a genius!

There is price to pay for genius
Mine is, my dislocation
From my world,
My estrangement from it.

But I now innately,
Vitally,
Critically am harmonized
With every aspect of the universe
Whether that harmony is acknowledged,
Or not,
And I am at peace
In my inward,
Because genius
The child-like state
And greatness,
Are states of harmony!

MEANING...

If there is anything
In this universe,
It has meaning
Any action,
Thought,
Word,
Any physical reality

And any eventuality,
Like schizophrenia
It has to have meaning

This is an invitation
To a multi-coloured world,
Of immense variety,
Which if shorn of the distress
That accompanies it,
Would inform
And develop the world
In every sphere of human activity
Science, the arts,
And spirituality

Science, because,
The rapidity and efficiency
And accuracy
Of intellectual processing
Possessed by someone with schizophrenia
Is superior to that of any scientist
Not afflicted by this malady;

The speed of thinking on science,
And ability to process information
Available to someone
Afflicted with schizophrenia,
Allied to appropriate subject matter
And a concerned approach
Would yield dividends
In scientific knowledge
Hitherto unprecedented –
It would be the foundation
Of a new, successful thinking
In science research –
And multiply the range of attitudes

And variety of endeavour
Undertaken by the scientist

The arts
Would be influenced for the better
By schizophrenia,
Again, by the ability
Of the heart and mind
Of the client
To associate,
With meaning
And content,
Images,
Concepts,
Ideas,
Feeling,
Emotions
In an imaginative manner –
The association of a disparate
Range of source-information
Into an arrangement
Genuinely artistic,

With form,
And greatly meaningful

The arts
Would be taken further
By schizophrenia's thinking
A journey far, far, further
Than the 'conventional' artist can
undertake –

Spirituality, and spiritual acumen
And knowledge,
Will be furthered,
By the heart and mind
Of the person afflicted,
Because the inner state
Of schizophrenia
Is a naturally concentrated one
It is a deep immersion
Into a truly, genuinely, spiritual world,
And thus spiritual facts
Are ready, at hand
And schizophrenia
Is such a fruitful
And fertile zone
For spirituality
That the fruits
Of a rich spiritual world
Are a torrential outpouring,

That can truly become,
If managed well,
A copious shower
Of spiritual knowledge –

This is the vast,
Rich realm,
A plentiful inner world
That the client
Is introduced to
By dint of having schizophrenia –
The prescription?

Physicians hark!

You, the doctors,
Need to quell the distress
Suffered by the client,
But not subdue
And unduly suppress
The imagination
And the stream of knowledge
Issuing from the client's
Mind
And as eventually happens,
His or her heart

The pain is to be alleviated,
But their mental processes
Are to be kept sacrosanct

In this fashion,
The physician
Can reduce the pain of dislocation
Suffered by the client,
But not his or her newly acquired –
Vivid and brilliant

Ability with colourful mental imagery
This brightest of faculties
May be re-acquired,
If we talk of relapses

But this tremendous, energetic
Prowess
Is to be nurtured,
Using appropriate medication
And not annulled –

The world only stands to gain
If psychiatry was to re-orient
Its chemical stance
Held towards the client,

And enable,
Not the cessation
Of his or her precious mentality,
But a nourishing,
Sustenance
And cherishing of it

The world
Of the arts, sciences
And spirituality
Will be the greater for it.

SURFACE...

The surface, 'perceived' of, says:

'A being completely annulled;
'A being of no consequence;
'A man who won't witness significance;
'An inarticulate man,
'with nothing to say;
'A person with a poor inner universe;
'Someone with little or no capacity;
'Someone without a meaningful history,
'and no consequential biography;
'An absolutely basic human being;
'He will never be skilled;
'He cannot visualize;
'His life is minimal,
'with no real drama;
'He makes no impact –
'he is easily forgotten;
'He has known no intellectual
development,
'and alas, never will
'thus he has no vantage;

'He knows nothing;
'He can never be original;
'An unattractive person;
'A most mediocre person;
'This man is very thick.'

So thinks the new person in my life
A stranger
A new young member of staff
At the library I have been frequenting
Since exit from hospital
After being sectioned –
I am young, like her
And this is her evaluation,
I judge,
When I think,
After several encounters,
About her attitude to me

This is how new people I come across
Summarize me now-a-days,

After a little experience
of my personality.

She is attractive looking,
So I am drawn to her,
An attraction hopeless of result;

For I am right now,
Inconsequential
In every department of existence
Rendered so;
The desertion of everything
That could accomplish positive result
Has occurred to me, utterly so;

But I have access to magic,
And can perform the magician's art
The foundation of which
Is aspiration and ambition

I will turn the summary
Of these new people
Who come into my life around
And that of those near to me
I will transform it,
For I am a magician,
With the magician's skills

And paraphernalia
And I will put both into action:
For, I will keep love in my heart;
I will successfully exercise
A protracted, bitter patience,
For years if necessary;
I will not be prey to bitterness;
I will not give in to despair;
I will be constantly positive
In thought,
Word
And action;
My willpower will be implacable,
Never to be unhinged;
I will be resigned,
Contented with my lot;
I will find purpose
Study,
And I have a vision
I concentrate upon realizing
University;

I witness then, already,

From a rich angle of vision
Multiple angles

My aspiration, university;
My patience;
My endeaour to be of good character;
And I resume my comeback everyday:
A habitual practice of niceness
Certainly keeping goodwill in my heart,
Though it may not
be possible to express it;

I strive through a knowledge base –
For I strive to gain learning
By reading voraciously;
And I continue apace:
To observe the world
of personal learning –
Its styles, manners,
system and methods,
For an aspect of my vision,
Aspiration and ambition

Is to be a genuine scholar –
The gel that brings all
my yearning together

Is my perennial patience
And so I continue, consistently,

Patiently,
With faith and self-belief
With the passage of years –

Eight years later,
I have a Dip H. E. and a BSc.

Now those with a short
experience of me,
Strangers who come into my life,
And those near to me, say:

'A being reaching accomplishment,
'Near complete fulfilment;
'A truly relevant individual
for our times;
'A tremendously articulate person
'with a most fertile, resourceful mind;

'Someone with an immense
and rich inner world,
'and a great destiny;
'We feel that he has
a profound vision –
'We wonder at the great secret
'on which is based his

capacity to visualize;
'He is truly an evolved being;
"One of the most naturally talented
'people I have ever known";

'A man with a vast array of
the brightest offerings;
'A story the stuff of legend;
'What a rich, wonderful personality,
'It would fascinate to learn
'The content and trajectory
'of his intellectual and
personal development;
'His take on matters thoughtful
'is both original and deep;'
'He's made an impact on me
I will never forget;

Women now sometimes
find me attractive;
I cannot be further from mediocrity;
I am deemed brilliant;

I will though, never, never, forget
That I was once cast to ignominy
And irrelevance,

As inconsequential
As a human being
Assigned a lowly station in life,
Assigned a permanent low station

The world of adults,
I have learnt through this experience,
Is a superficial one;

And those who thought me ignominious,
And irrelevant
Are to me superfluous
And quite negligible to my needs

Not so the great nurses,
And brilliant mental health workers
Who yet upheld
A meaningful and significant future
For me, when sick
And profoundly disabled –

These deep nurses
And profound mental health workers
Are to me, heroic.

If I was made stark and bare once,
After being sectioned,
The tree of my life
Became abundant with foliage

And fruit
And honour
In one distant, but
certain-to-come day
In the future

It requires magic and a magician
To conduct such a transformation –
With basic, but brilliant qualities
Utilized by someone rendered basic –
But yet human – very human – qualities:

Being made very human then
I used the very human
quality of patience
To guide me to the resting place
I so yearned for:
It is difficult to learn
the magician's art

And to be a true magician –
But it lies in being very human,

And I suppose you are
only very human
When you are rendered low,
Basic
And heartbroken.

ACHIEVEMENT

I say,
To receive schizophrenia
In one's heart and mind
Is to attain vastly –

For, have I not come unto
A new, uncharted universe,
Hitherto unperceived,
Or experienced,
By any other human,
An original world
With unique meaning?

That I needed to hold onto
This primal universe,
Minus my perturbation,
Was something beyond the ken
Of psychiatric science,
Which suppressed,
With chemicals,
This flourishing inner world,
And took away all thought from me

The terrifying,
As well as the edifying

The chemical regime,
By its institution,
Makes itself thereafter indispensable,
Or you re-call the entire experience,
Of which, to science,
The thoughts that are wayward
Are those to home in upon
Not the creative spirit
That schizophrenia fosters,
Which alas, is bludgeoned

Yet, deprived of a kingdom
Of real heart and soul
The true heart and soul

A rich flourishing kingdom
That, initiated by the malady,
Now belongs to you innately,
But is rescinded from you
By mechanistic psychiatry,
There are yet attainments
You garner,

Amid the convulsive life
Left behind,
Amid the debris
Of a shattered inner world
Pulped and mashed by medication

For troubles have come to me,
With a permanent stalling,
And to wake up to this blight,
And still try to maintain equanimity
Is a real attainment;

Every single positive thought,
Word
And action
Attain significance now;

To keep your eyes open,
And gaze forwards,
With hope
And great expectations
Are in the same vein;

To want to show affection
Is a tremendous departure
For one so hamstrung,

And to actually portray it
Is an immense quality;

To attempt to make sense
Of what has befallen you,

In the light of hope,
And good character
To try to evoke therefore,
A unique philosophy
Is salutary indeed;

This positive nature
Is symptomatic
Of a magnified heart
The heart of someone
with schizophrenia

Is it not unexpected
By the world,
And fantastic,
That someone so reduced

By a catastrophic illness
Can will into being and
Can possess an amplified heart?

The heart is the seat
Of the greatness
Of the client with schizophrenia,
And since greatness is necessary
To deal effectively with this condition,
The psychiatrist's focus
Ought to be the client's heart

And not his physical brain,
Treated mechanistically,
With a chemical screw-driver?
It needs knowledge of spirituality
To deal with schizophrenia,
Not so much biochemistry
Though we need medication
To allay distress

All said and done,
The fact that the client,

Even after medical treatment,
Possesses, deep down,
A flourishing spiritual world,
Is to say that he or she is wealthy –

And then when you consider
Their positive dealings with
The aftermath of hospital events,
These –
A rich spiritual attainment,
And an immense visualization
of hope
All these –

Make schizophrenia
An event that is an achievement!

THE MEANING AND RAMIFICATION OF SCHIZOPHRENIA

At nineteen I was severely disabled, by paranoid schizophrenia, in both personality and intellect. I couldn't even count numerically. But, I exercised patience and recovered both in personality and intellect to succeed at university.

I graduated for the second time in 1986. I felt again after a recent relapse – June 2018 – and further ill health – that I could not impress anymore – and I did not. But to impress the world – what does that truly mean and amount to? I need to impress God and the Prophet Muhammad, upon whom be peace.

And these both look at the core and essence of me – the real me, where I am a great individual.

I need a wife that can witness the core and essence of me – and there are very few women who can do this.

In my essence, I am not disabled – and in the heart and mind of the Prophet Muhammad, and in the Eyes and Heart of God, I am complete and completed.

And this Divine verdict is the most important one to me, far, far outweighing the world's interpretation and judgment of me.

I am disabled in the world, and my detractors enjoy this fact. But from the Divine point of view, I am whole.

This truth feels better than supressing and defeating my ego.

**On the path of Love,
To be awake is the prerequisite.
But I had to learn this lesson.
My particular difficulty
Schizophrenia**

Put me into sleep
A long time ago.

If I'd been awake,
After embracing the path
In the forty-plus years
Intervening my being put to sleep
And my attempt to wake up,
I would have been constantly
God-conscious.
I would Love have accrued greatly –
Alas!
I couldn't have woken up –
I was debarred from this wakening –
I was too much –
Much too much –
Unconscious.

Now, at 58,
Even at this late stage,
Once again,
I try to shake off the slumber.

It is like being released
From long imprisonment,
And hence hard to adjust to,

And habituate to.
The path of Love
I have always discovered
Strewn with thorns,
And it is so today –
I am encumbered
By what yet needs doing.

But, I now, at 58, realize
That Love's design
Is consummate –
It gives
Where it most takes –

The Ear of the Universe
Belongs to my cries;
The Heart of the Universe
Loves me,
And has Loved me greatly,
At every instance:

And I feel this great Love
In my heart
With all its meaning
And ramification.

Though bereft –
Practically –
For all outward purposes,

Inwardly
I am wholly intact.
My desires
And wishes
Are the Universe's desires
And wishes.

Love was, and is,
The complete panacea
To all my prayers –
For the beleaguered world,
For every tyranny and oppression –
Through every age –
And the cruelty of man
In general.

My prayers
Have been wholly accepted
By Love.
In this acceptance,
I find my freedom –

The most vital
And critical occurrence
In my whole life.

This is *one – one - single item* of news
From the Universe of Love,
The greatest
And finest
Fact
Of the created cosmic universe.

THANK YOU!

SHAKIL A I DAWOOD

IMMERSIONS
'THE OCEAN'

THE POETRY OF SCHIZOPHRENIA AND PSYCHOSIS

VOLUME 3

KINDLE DIRECT PUBLISHING

BOOKS BY SHAKIL A I DAWOOD

THE 500 COMPLETE TWO LINE   POEMS

A SPEAR OF GRASS POETRY

IN CONTEMPLATION   SELECTED POETRY

GRIEF AND GOD

THE HAIRDRESSERS SALON

A SPIRITUAL ANTIDOTE TO DEPRESSION

KALAM THE PEN

OBSERVATIONS: A LIFE EXPERIENCED

IMMERSIONS POEMS

THE VERSE GARLANDS

GOODNESS KINDNESS AND LOVE

ASPECTS OF THE HEART VOL 1

ASPECTS OF THE HEART VOL 2

**'WORDS'   ESSAYS ON
LIVING WITH SCHIZOPHRENIA**

TO THOSE WHO SPEAK KINDLY POEMS

INVITE THE DIVINE   POEMS

WITNESSING   MESSAGES OF HOPE

THE CAFÉ OF LOVE SELCTED POEMS

'IMMERSIONS,
THE POETRY OF SCHIZOPHRENIA
AND PSYCHOSIS' VOLUMES I AND 2

'SOLACE IN A MAELSTROM,
CONVERSATIONS WITH GOD'

'ART THERAPY FOR SCHIZOPHRENIA,
A NOVEL APPROACH'

'OBSERVATIONS OF THE PROPHETS:
THEIR CHARACTERS AND PERSONALITIES'

'REVOLUTIONARY POEMS,
AN EFFECTIVE GUIDE TO
NON-VIOLENT INSURRECTION'

THANK YOU!

YH YMm YAMkm